Jab Jage Tab Savera

Orange Books Publication

1st Floor, Rajhans Arcade, Mall Road, Kohka, Bhilai, Chhattisgarh 490020
Website: **www.orangebooks.in**

First Edition, 2025

ISBN: 978-93-7426-771-4

Price: Rs. 399.00

Printed in India

Jab Jage Tab Savera

Chayan Ghosh

Orange Books Publication
www.orangebooks.in

Index

Ordinary vs. Genius

Genius is born in intervals and always by choice. This is the reason why they are few in number. It is said that the ALMIGHTY GOD felt dismay at his own creation. Why? Because God is a salesperson, and that too a super salesperson. God does not like to drift away from his own superior salesmanship image by his own creations. The newborn genius challenges him, repeatedly, and the challenges are so brutal that god's self-created integrity becomes brittle after each shock attack. Therefore, God becomes alert and smart to narrow down his mistakes to zero mistakes. Therefore, genius is very rare nowadays among the millions of his ordinary creations. When the ordinary is more in number and genius is a few, the battle is lost, though the real battle is won by the almighty, by displaying his creative skills and selfishness, which is a sign of a smart salesperson. God has also screwed the ordinary one's scoring ability into blanks and far less venomous and spineless in the near future. However, a battle once lost or won is temporary. It is an unending process. Maybe God is overconfident and overambitious in his thoughts, which pays heavily to his masterful salesmanship crafts. Once the situation changes, the ordinary one becomes flamboyant and throws countless challenges at him, and thus, a new era starts. It is a thrill to notice that when millions of ordinary ones roar like lightning, the almighty gets dumb. Millions of light - years may take the events to happen, but it has finally happened. When it happens, a happy journey begins when the ordinary ones are in the race and the future promises to be promising for them.

It is a process of great evolution through the ages which turns yesterday's ordinary ones into today's visionaries. Endless their name, unending their fame, as you know all of them, it matters only to you, tame. Get out of your prison. Drag your head towards the horizon. Do not bother about the season. Succeed in eluding all excuses and reasons. A poet, in his poetic sense, will not find anything great there, because it is not a good poem, but each ordinary one will accept it by their soul. It is a mantra, an elixir for building up the mindset. It is a jihad to demolish the concrete walls of self-created depression and limitations. To earn the status of one of the strongest mind settlers, one need not visit the Himalayan cave and stay there for years together. It can be achieved at one's own sweet home, and that too without any cost. Just one has to rediscover oneself by taking enough water and oxygen freely available in nature, because both these agents purify the mind, body and soul and enrich every cell. It may be a bit late for someone. However, as it is said, "Better late than never." One may wake up at 1 pm; however, it is said **JAB JAGE TAB SAVERA.**

Start giving a new and fresh look to every cell of your body, as cells are the basic unit of life; let all the cells grow faster than before to replenish dead cells. Though it is a mandatory process of life, the growth of healthy cells in life copes with the adversity of life in a better way. That is the keyhole of a clock room, banked with billions of dollars. Is there anybody who does not want to be a billionaire on this earth? Ironically, only a few were able to make a hole in it. Why is it so? It is because there is a light - year gap between intention and action.

Intention vs. Action

It is said that intention and action are two opposite forces acting in opposite directions. Hence, the resultant effect is zero. That is why most people never taste the flavour of success in their life, despite of their good intentions. The reason can be attributed to the fact that our brain is a good conductor of heat. It charges very fast. When a person is hurt, the brain is heated. Emotions like outbursts and violent screaming are all reactions of the heated brain.

However, we all know that things which charge fast also discharge fast. As such, outburst and violent screaming is followed by depression and sobbing. It is a universal truth that when a dear one lives no more, the closest person cries and sobs, but there are also a few instances where the nearest ones are forced to cry and sob to neutralise their mind. Or else there remains the risk of the brain to skid.

It was earlier thought, intentions are inputs and actions are outputs. Therefore, if one focuses on good input, the output should be good. However, in reality, it does not always happen. This paradox is due to the fact that intentions and actions are both inputs. However, most people misunderstand considering action to be an output. Just as if without fuel, an engine is useless, in the same way without action, the intention has no use.

Strategy vs. Implementation

The two words Intention and action have lost their sharp edge owing to their overusage and that's why two new words have replaced them. They are strategy and implementation. The corporate offices of all the top business houses globally are pouring out newer and newer strategies every day and getting themselves involved in debates about how the best strategy can be implemented. There are tons of papers published in support of successful strategy and ideal implementation, but it is inevitable to learn that no strategy is 100% perfect and all accept its implementation procedure. It is because nobody in this world has yet mastered both the art, and no one knows if it is achievable at all or not. Therefore, the experiment continues.

Intention is a state of mental status having weak and strong wavelengths, which vary from one to another. A physically weak and handicapped person belongs to a strong wavelength, may be gifted by his creator. In contrast, a physically strong and sound person has a comparatively weak wavelength. When experimented it is learnt that both these qualities are inbuilt and stay lifelong unless external forces demagnetise their own path (course). These external forces act on both physically weak and strong person throughout their life and are directly proportional to. To a physically disabled person, the external opposite forces are big one to neutralise the strong wavelength, whereas to a physically capable person, the external forces are small enough to neutralise the weak wavelength. It is said that when the situation is tough, only the tough are through. Nobody wants to die, however physically weak one may be. To survive, a weak person has to fight a do-or-die battle to counter the external challenges in keeping the strong wavelength intact. A blind person could well recognise his friends and foes more than a visually sound person could by his divine sense, specially composed of complex genes and active hormones. In order to acquire this magic power, one has to solve several mysteries of a tiny life which remain unsolved by millions of people who never ever live a life throughout their lifespan and thus remain unmarked. The mystery of life is like the mystery of the universe and space. The more you go through, the more you inflame your eyebrow. Still, to raise one's standard, one has to solve certain mysteries in life. To attain a certain height of standard in life, it is necessary to solve certain numbers of mystery of life, and it is equal or the same to all levels of people, irrespective of strong and weak physiques. It matters little whether one hails from a royal family or not. However, what really matters is how one has fought his life's royal battle to earn his own distinction like a highly devoted and disciplined soldier. Mystery of life torched his own hideout only to the bravest dignitaries of the world who have dared to challenge him. It is like taming a mad horse by a skilled master. Only those who can conquer the uneven battle at the cost of sheer willpower, the goddess of life garlanded them.

Battle, Battle, Battle. Life is full of battles in every sphere. Now what for this battle? Someone says that for existence. Only for existence, it is a wrong attitude. Never do that. Battle is for one's own top identity. As we all know that after 80,000 lives, one gets a human life. How precious it is! So, nurture your life through battles; there is no other alternative available. So what else can one do? Never say goodbye, battle, enough. There is no satisfaction limit, there is no success limit. Only the sky is the limit. Because a man lives with battle and dies with battle. No one can escape. One must be thrilled to know that in one second of life, how much battle has to be performed by one's heart and the other biological systems. So when one's own system is battling, how could one leave a battle?

When one's own body system is battling every second to keep one's valuable organs fresh, healthy, and ever smart, how can one then wish to leave the battlefield?

What is the necessity of a battle? It is said that whenever an external challenge arises, a battle ensues. It is the only way to prove one's superiority. As every person living on earth is mercilessly challenged, one has no other way but to demolish the threat through battle. When there is a battle, only one wins. However, the one who wins does not win forever. Because the one who loses gathers courage and learns better skills than before in due course of time and thus throws another challenge.

Therefore, the previous winner has to develop more courage and lethal skills to overcome this ongoing challenge to stay as a winner. It is important here to notice that one cannot fight a battle of tomorrow with yesterday's systems and skills. That is why continuous development is necessary. One must be kept updated with the latest skills and techniques.

Our own body system is built with an in-built defence system. There are numerous defence systems as alert as ever guarding our most valuable organs through battle as long as we remain alive. Our defence system, when battle produces a necessary amount of antibodies to counter the external challenge, and when any foreign agent tries to invade our systems, the antibodies fight with it. In a battle, one has to win, so if the antibody wins, foreign agents are destroyed, and our body systems remain agile as before. However, if the foreign invader wins the battle, destroying the antibody protein, our body system loses its ability, and thus it requires input antibody from outside, which we call medicines.

One thing that has to be noticed in our body system, not all the millions of daily activities wait for their boss's order or their mere presence to start their activities. Thus, the boss in our body system is a wrong concept. whom should one crown this honour ? Brain, heart, nervous system, blood, enzymes, hormones, gastric juices, lungs, kidneys, genes or cells, no one is ideal. Every agent is a boss and possesses sound skills to perform their own jobs. In performing the job, they found it challenging.

Like that in one's battle, one need not wait for his boss to start one's job. It is rightly said that neither a boss wishes to work for his juniors nor a junior wishes to work for his boss. In this selfish world, when a boss works, he is working for his own career and prosperity. And not for his juniors. If anybody pretends that one is working for the other, it is a big lie. Would anybody believe a liar or a hypocrite? Most interestingly, millions of liars and hypocrites are living on this earth at the cost of millions of unfortunates. Neither have they fled away from the battlefield nor have they lost in the battlefield, but in the actual way of life, they never received anything.

Try to enjoy a life full of battles, and if you can, you have already won half of those battles. Never complain about the battle and seek help from others. You will get nothing. When your nearest kin are battling, how is it possible for them to lend support to you? Do not be depressed. Do not misunderstand anybody, at any point in your life. You will be in a better position if you do not trust anyone other than yourself. Never dream that your nearest kin will stand beside you in your greatest battles. In addition, why should they? Are you helpless? If you think or project yourself as helpless, certainly you need not bother to live on this earth. You have no right to do that.

Whom do you curse? Your parents? Family? Relatives? Religion? Society? Village? Town? Country? Friends and foes? Your nearest ones and the strangers are not the real cause of your adversity. If there is any doubt, you are allowed to question anyone. However, you will never get your answer anywhere. Maybe some of your learned friends will try to show you the Milky Way by saying, "Do this and don't do that". However, no one will do anything on your behalf. That is why if you have no friends or well-wishers in your life, never waste a second of your time thinking about them. A lonely life is better than a bunch of unfruitful friends. However, is it possible to live a life of solitude? Has any man achieved anything big in life by staying alone? The answer is a straight YES. Because people who achieve big things in life on their own were different, are different and will be different from the general mass. When you are alone, you do perceive things differently, and this ability to perceive things differently takes you towards a new beginning. The agony of loneliness builds a pressure inside your body, it pulls you to a great height, and thus your thinking, the latent energy and the vision power become magnified. In addition, you will be in a position to align your thinking with your action perfectly by converting the latent energy into kinetic energy. All of us know that to achieve something very big in our lives, we have to think big first. However, is it so? Not at all. Only 1% of the total earthly population thinks big at first and then achieves it. They are being labelled as greats, legends, the effect of genetic advantage and whatnot. Nevertheless, don't you feel you also have the same potential? Yes, you have to feel first. Always keep thinking big about yourself and your strength by burying all of your weaknesses under the Pacific Ocean. Dream you are very big, day and night, talk to yourself always, but never talk to others, for it will certainly jeopardise your mindset. Rest assured that one day you will be adjudged as GREAT.

It is certain that when you do this, by seeing your changing behaviour, people will say something about you. Even people who never worried about you or recognised you will start taking an interest on you. You were never their concern, but suddenly, due to some unknown attraction, which you are now radiating, beats others. It is a kind of sensation, which is well known as envy. Nobody wants to see you achieve greatness; nobody wants you to succeed in life. Nobody will be able to digest your new standard of living. All these result in hatred and envy, and those people may even label you as "Mad". You will be surprised to note that to whom you were dear yesterday, today you become a devil. What harm did you do to them? Nothing. What wrong have you done by lifting your standard and position? All your dearest and nearest ones were happy to see you, tiny, tame, cowardly, poor, uneducated, helpless, below average, dishonest, thief, liar. You were the centre of their coffee shop gossip. You were the self-signed cheque for all the entertainment and refreshment of your friends, society and your town enjoyed at your cost.

How long will you be able to sustain your agonies by doing so? You might be thinking, "What a tiny man like me could do?" However, that is the game. Put the question to yourself about all the greats of the universe, who were actually small that walked the earth before you. Try to locate them, their size and their shape and the attributes that led to their greatness. Try to find out their source of motivation. Keep searching for the answers until you can relate them to yourself. Spend some time sitting near a big temple or a big mountain, or a big river and try to connect yourself with your surroundings. You will be surprised to receive valuable wisdom from them. Preserve and perceive those wisdom and you will get the answer to your life's melancholy. You will get the answer about how to deal with them and the steps you will have to take to see you through. Once you are through, you will be able to feel the pulse of it. Fasten your energy belt and drive yourself towards a long journey of success. You will be surprised to note that you are being driven by a very high magnitude of speed and direction when others never ever thought of dreaming it. Gradually, you will be able to upgrade yourself. A standard, which was unknown to you, will welcome you. Accept the opportunities of your upgradation like a satellite station, make a base there and try to see down from there. You will be surprised to acknowledge that all the big hurdles you once thought to be unconquerable now look like an easy pole vault jump. In addition, the people whom you thought to be Goliath were actually small in reality.

This is a sincere and not a very difficult proposition, which you had earlier neglected, many a time and truly by a man of millions, is by landing oneself.

However, you have to pay to earn success. What do you to pay and what is the cost? May I ask you what the cost you had to pay to earn this human life? Certainly, it was very high. Because it was 80,000 lives after. May I ask you how much it cost your beloved mother to bring you into this world? Certainly, the pain she bore was very costly indeed. Your beloved father might have prayed thousands of times to the Almighty to get you as a child. Therefore, you have to pay a high price to repay the debt of your birth. Think about it, and you will notice the inner voice. You will hear it without an ounce of doubt, but only when you make it audible to yourself with your intuition. Everybody possesses it, including you. But you have to develop the ability to listen to it. Just as if one has to pay cash to make a demand draft, such is the nature of possessing the sixth sense.

You might think it to be difficult to accomplish. In addition, indeed it is. Because to accomplish something, a person has to work very hard, and you are not an exception. The latest formulae to get big success in life is by landing oneself in no man's land. If one has the courage and the zeal, only then can one take his position in the starting block of the sprint. Sometimes people tend to get bored and depressed, and may lose their own identity. That is a very tragic conclusion to their life. Most people disappoint themselves by glorifying their negligible achievements and live their lives by age and not by deeds. The world will not fall too. One is the master of his own will, soul and future, and in no way should be disturbed. It is fine for a person to be happy if the person thinks that his clerical job of thirty-five years in a bank is a huge achievement. Moreover, I should not and must not spite him for his thinking. However, I will neither counsel him that it is one of the few bare minimum achievements in a person's life. Because if I did, I would lead a life of scary uncertainties, and who knows, it might bury me eventually.

What my wisdom says is to lead a life free of uncertainties rather than a life full of them. As we all know that there are uncertainties in every phase of life. No one is fortunate enough to run away from it. So whenever there is a remote possibility of avoiding them, one should confront them with courage and spirit, and this is the best way to deal with them. The better you become in acquiring the skill for dealing with uncertainties, the less is the chance of them picking your life.

Millions of ordinary people are afraid to take risks in their lives. This fear is solely responsible for crushing their prospects and opportunities. As prospects and opportunities are very competitive, if one fails to grab them because of their fear of taking risks, those prospects and opportunities may be lost forever. It has happened thousands of times, and wise person has taken lessons from it. The most important lesson is that when one is afraid of taking risks in their life, they are actually risking all the good things from happening in their life.

This is a universal truth. Equally important is avoiding taking too many reckless risks in life. One can question what kind of risk one should take. The answer is indeed very simple. One should take a calculated risk. Is the explanation clear? If not, then here is the explanation. Suppose a high jump professional could jump one meter in his first attempt during a competition. Then he should target one and a half meters in his second attempt and not two meters. This is called calculative risk. It has been proven again and again that when a calculative risk is taken, the failure percentage is a mere 10%. What I am trying to state here is that when calculative risks are taken, the success percentage is around 90%. The percentage keeps on fluctuating when one becomes more cautious about the risk taken. However, overcalculating risk is dangerous just like overconfidence and can prove to be too costly a mistake. So proper care has to be taken while taking calculative risks and should be planned meticulously before implementation.

There is a mad rush among people when it comes to framing strategies without knowing much about their fate . It is because neither are they healthy and wealthy at birth. There is not a single instance where it happens anywhere in the world. Why is it so? If it were not, then it would be reckoned as a heavenly task, which only GOD could perform. However, as human beings are devoid of such skills, success is achieved after a long, tenacious battle. The prime factor is the TIME. A strategy put forward to achieve a certain height has to be time-framed, for the more time it consumes, the lesser is the rate of success. A strategy is rated by its virtue of its successful returns, divided by time. Strategy may be discovered or invented. However, discovering a strategy is more difficult than inventing it. Too hard, when observed from the point of TIME, it consumes the investment that is required. A strategy founder may find it lucrative to rediscover an old strategy, but it will not be easy for him to give proper shape it requires by external forces because old is not always gold and a bold motivation is hard to get hold of. Such is the risk that of old is gold strategy to date remains buried, and the trend is to look for newer and newer strategies. The trend is good and should be welcomed. When a strategy, after implementation, could not yield the desired result, it should be dropped immediately. Trying in vain to improvise it lessens the success rate.

It is not compulsory to formulate the finest strategy to attain a good success rate because it is costly and time-consuming. During strategy formulation, it should always be kept in mind that more simpler the strategy is, more easily it will be to implement and the higher the success rate with utilisation of lesser cost and time. It is not a logic but a theory. First, a strategy founder should not hire; he should be an inherent property of a molecule, and he should understand its Mass, valency, electrons of his own men. Secondly, he should be able to estimate the strength and weakness of his own means. When these two parameters converge with one another at a point and form a right angle, there are chances of success.

Unfortunately, 99% of today's strategies take birth and die at infancy due to carelessness in their manoeuvre. Thus, taking great care in manoeuvring a strategy can prevent a big loss. What is the big loss? The big loss is the image portfolio. Because once you lose your image, it can take years to rebuild it. In addition, if you try to put the world's latest and top - class strategy to rebuild it, it might end up yielding a very low success rate, and thereby it will be in vain to attempt to put life into a dead body. Therefore, a dead body's rightful place is in the graveyard, and no light of success can ever reach it.

From darkness to light and then again back to the darkness is the life cycle of a strategy. As if a strategy takes birth, it governs, and then it is dethroned. Hence, a strategy has a life of its own. That is why, to get maximum mileage, a strategy should be implemented with great speed and velocity.

Repeatedly, it has been noticed that though the strategies were new and fresh, the people who were supposed to implement them were shabby compared to the founding partners. As the founder partners were not able to take part in the implementation process, it is unworthy to call them a catalyst. However, if by chance, the founder partner becomes worthy to become a catalyst, the byproduct or the result becomes astonishing. But the chances for it to happen are very rare, with a possibility that counts to one millionth of a fraction. It is not an odd one, but in real practice, it is said to be normal. It can never be a one-man show, and it should not be.

Strategy founder and strategy implementer are two separate identities, and thus, it require a fellow feeling between the two, which is of paramount importance. It is like a baby in the mother's womb tied up to her by the umbilical cord. A mother here therefore plays the role of a strategy founder who has to send nutrition through the umbilical cord to the baby, who acts like the strategy implementer. To give birth to a healthy baby, a mother gives up everything for around 36 weeks, forgetting each painful second of her life. Similarly, a strategy founder has no other option but to sacrifice everything towards a noble cause. Is it an easy job and can everyone pull it through? If it is so, then why do we find people lamenting in every corner of the world?

It is virtually an impossible task that has been proved not once but on several occasions. However, why is it an impossible task? It is because of the complex system put forward by the strategy founders. For example, 2+2+2+2=8 and 2^3=8. Both are systems, and both are correct, but which is the simpler one? Anybody can easily guess and understand it. However, for a strategy founder, 2+2+2+2=8 is more time-consuming compared to 2^3=8. Therefore, they impose it on the implementer partner. It is experimentally that most of them could not find a solution to 2^3=8 as they could easily find for 2+2+2+2=8, but it is a matter of regret that there is nobody to say that both are only systems and their contents are the same.

Many times, lack of communication stands between the success and failure of a strategy and thus a civil war starts between them, killing the whole motivation. Both indulge in harmful acts, thus spoiling the spirit. Therefore, in the end, the strategy becomes the victim of the devil spirit that tears it through and through. However, who ends up as the winner? It is obvious the answer is the devil spirit. However, is there any way to guess it at its inception? Devil spirits haunt only in the darkness. Just like a shiny day and a rainy day are always better than a cloudy day, so is a cloudy day with high humidity messes up the whole proceedings.

Implementation of a strategy in a disciplined manner is always a big ask and chances of error are less. The whole activity is under duress because of torrid times. Thus, before implementing a strategy, it should be thoroughly understood and in every phase and step, corrective measures should be taken immediately. Understanding a strategy requires sense and grabbing power. In order to do it, it is better to formulate it in simple implementation languages. Probably the best language they understand without consuming too much time in debate and consultation. It is thus a challenge for a strategy developer to develop some languages that reward itself for their own cause.

Now what is that language? In one sense, language means communication, and in another sense, is pronunciation. Both things have to be well coordinated. How can it be done? It can be done when only certain measures are taken care of, like free and fair opportunities, equal benefits and rights, lesser threats and less pressure. Above all, it should be acknowledged with prizes.

When we talk about free and fair opportunities during implementation, it is not like that in all phases and steps, each one of them will be incorporated. Here, the choice lies with the implementer. The implementer will be able to draw his own involvement in a variety of options rather than it being imposed against his will.

It should be announced before strategy implementation that whatever revenue the strategy earns would be equally divided among the different stakeholders.

Similarly, if the strategy fails to earn revenue, the responsibility of failure should all be borne by all the stakeholders equally?

All the above-mentioned points speak about a network system well-knit by an organised team. After all, it is teamwork.

Millions of successful implementers still living here have first received acknowledgement for their success, but were never awarded anything. Why? Because they are only implementers and not the founders of the strategy. When benefits and financial awards are given to the strategy founders for the success of the strategy, the strategy implementers receive only a certificate.

Ironically, not only were the strategy implementers deprived of benefits and financial awards, but they were also held responsible for the failure of the strategy. The world was then shocked to notice that they were not recognised as a team. It is because when one group is awarded for the success, the other group is deprived. Therefore, a well-knit team is divided into pieces and thus loses the intensity, speed, and velocity, the core factors required to make a strategy successful. Therefore, everywhere a team is divided into groups that fight among each other, weakening the proceedings. In many organisations, this infighting happens under the dark enabling the devil spirit to kill the whole effort.

Ever since this prejudice existed, the situation remained unchanged. In addition, ever seen the right cause to identify their credibility ruins its prospect. Incredibility denotes a wrong notion, and that to in a crunch situation where there is little time to look back and repair the damage, it froze the pendulum of the clock.

Even though all these factors are easily noticeable and repairable, it demands a positive, brave will to correct them. The very thinnest groups in our universe can notice and smell the foul odour but fail to take detailed measures to repair it. Maybe they had to take some risks and uncertainties to do that, but that is the most basic cost one has to pay. However, who will bell the cat? The bravest person in the world will have to think twice to implement it. That person has ample time to think, but he has no Godfather. If he does, he will be named as the first man on this earth, but there are many hurdles to pass.

The first hurdle is the fear of defamation. Fame is well accepted by all, but defamation is not. A person runs his whole life after fame to be famous and pompous, but is against running after defamation. Maybe because people will end up calling him mad, a very unpopular word everyone likes to wheeze past. It may be the ultimate risk one has to take.

The second hurdle is the fear of failure. It is common sense that no one likes to see others succeed, which propels them to live an uncomfortable life. When one compares his success with another and finds its gravity to be less, it strikes a failure of failure. It is a well-known fact that a projection of high success always returns a high failure in life. One may be the best in his faculty, he may be the best in his thinking and activity, but that does not guarantee him to be the biggest winner.

The third hurdle is the risk of developing others. It is the greatest risk one has to take to earn self-esteem and satisfaction. However, in reality, there is hardly anyone in this world to can give a lesson which is worthy of being taught to others. A lesson relies on a few basic things like auto reflex, self-styled act, self-innovation, speed, momentum, and accuracy. These are the autonomous traits of a rare personality. All these valuable possessions remain as a copyright of them. They can never be taken away from them in their lifetime. These are called inherent properties, but there are some basics, which can be acquired quite easily, such as discipline, punctuality, sincerity, and religiousness, that are equally important for the development of others. It is very painful to say that millions of people do not even know the real functioning of these basics, and when asked for lending some support, people do not put their best effort to earn their fundamentals. So some people end up having wrong fundamentals, which leads to their below-par performance.

The fourth hurdle is the risk of being caught, and the ultimate result is embarrassment as it is proven that no matter how perfect a human being is, he will always have some degree of deficiency and loopholes. Certain people, instead of correcting those deficiencies and loopholes, end up masking them. This may be due to their ego, which stops them from taking the necessary action. This acts like a cancer in the future and keeps troubling them. It is not a matter of ignorance but a habitual fault to find its remedy. This is what can be described as a tragedy of a great man. It was also noticed that when asked about the single odds, it was not given any great importance, as if there was nothing to do about it and thus it persists long enough to eventually hamper their loyalty and honesty. It is a kind of indifferent attitude, knowingly, whatever the reason that dilutes and arrests the vast potential. When estimated, it is learnt that it is also a kind of self-negative passion which burns some individuals into ashes. However, they are so strong in conception that they feel painful to discuss it with others, and thus throughout their life they carry it, until their last breath.

A simple job is performed by implementing a strategy, but the same cannot be said in the case of a difficult job. Why is it so? It is because a job is a sum. Strategy is the formula given and the steps followed to perform the sum based on the formula is the implementation. Now, if we take a simple sum like a simple factorisation, and it can be performed by a simple formula like $(a+b)^2$ or $(a+b)^3$, and its different steps to perform it are more or less simple. However, if the sum is a complex factorisation, it cannot be performed by using only one formula. It may require a combination of multiple formulae. Hence, based on simple formulae, complex algebra cannot be performed. Most of the time, the person behind the implementation of the strategy is vital. Just like a complex algebra problem requires a combination of formulas to solve it, in the same way, a difficult job requires a combination of strategies to get it done.

It is good to see that, when any strategy is framed, there exists a number of methodologies in its implementation to avoid certain numbers of difficulties. It is also proven that when it is practised the number of options given is not enough. Any brilliant strategy considered to have zero error could achieve at best only 20% of the desired result after its implementation. These strategies generating only 20% of the desired result are considered big flop. It can be compared to giant howitzer/bofors guns. It is not only a waste of financial resources but also a negative impact on the target, which unnecessarily causes a tremendous loss of life and property of the human race.

It is easily understood and decided that an off - target strategy is worse than having no strategy. Now, what is a no strategy? Strategy means formula, so a strategy means the absence of a formula in business. Algebraic, mathematical and geometrical sums require a formula, but there are sums which can be performed by simple procedures. They are the real basics of sum, whatever odds happen and are required by everybody doing simple calculations. Just as addition, subtraction, multiplication and division are easily done by simple procedure and any sum, whether algebraic, mathematical and geometrical, can't be done without them basics are taken here as common and is termed here "No" strategy is based on two very strong words, they are straight and easy. Straight means going up without any interruption, and the trend to go up is a smooth one. If we go deep into any strategy, we can locate how fast the strategy can be implemented from the starting point and, that too without any downward retardation. The other thing about strategy is that whatever odds come will not decrease its momentum. Thus, it requires a great force to accelerate and always maintain an average velocity, which demonstrates the smoothness of the strategy. It is understood that smoothness brings shine and glory and carries a comfortable position.

It is predicted that all good strategies adopted sincerely should emerge as a winner. It thus becomes a prestigious phenomenon when such important aspects are set to start. It is said that a good start always wins the race. Naturally, these factors are to be taken care of. So, starting the bloc/step of any strategy should be perfect. Strategy launch is comparable to a rocket launch. Therefore, it is imperative to think a hundred times before launching it. If not satisfied, it should be delayed. We have seen in the past that due to the faulty launch of a satellite/rocket, it could not reach its desired path and thus the whole effort went in vain, costing huge wastage of time and money. When such things occur, it drains our confidence and trust and develops a state of mental/physical inaptitude, jamming the whole affair.

Therefore, it is mandatory to take all precautionary measures to stop any such developments. Instead of taking all kinds of smart attention, a snag develops, and when detected, such snags should be corrected on an emergency basis, which eventually denies any loss of time. It is a general feeling that a timely start always brings mental satisfaction and a feeling of well-being. Therefore, if there is any delay in launch, a strong suspicion will arise, which will challenge its integrity ruthlessly. It is also observed that a delay in launch if fetches good results receive less appreciation and may be overlooked. Thus, to keep the strong feeling in favor, all strategies should be launched on time and produce the desired result for getting strong recognition.

It is a common practice that a few strategy bearers are very successful and remain always in front. Why is it so? It is because of strong, favourable sentiments and recognition. Many people thus believed that they were heavyweight in the business. In reality, those who were able to build such a rainbow spectrum made their task easy too. Therefore, it is very important to discharge such a twinkle spectrum, which is a trademark of success.

It is a simple task to make such a difficult subject easy due to the self-created success spectrum, which attracts the desired result. Thus, it is a strong belief that success attracts success, which is so important that it deserves other people's confidence automatically. It is like a stock exchange affair and becomes an automatic choice. As in the stock exchange, the biggest buyers of shares are the most trusted ones, so that a few strategy bearers act as a monopoly until something extraordinary misshapen.

If strategy is a theory, campaign is practical. A strategy without a campaign cannot walk. Similarly, a campaign without a specific strategy lies in duck. Therefore, it is vital to note that both parties are tied to each other, living by sharing wear and tear between them. They always remain flexible in receiving gifts at any interval. Possibly, there are no vacuums in building blocks.

Every piece of grey matter emphasises to do a hot and humid campaign, whatever the outside environment. Unless a campaign erupts with volcanic heat, the ice will not melt. So, a campaign has to feel the pulse and the meteorological pressure before it acts.

A campaign with its sharp teeth should acquire the skill of biting. It is like snakebite; one bite can kill the competitors. Its every bite is meant for beating its rivals, even though it is a situation of nail nail-biting finish.

However, not all the strategies are alike; they are different at the time of their conception and thus their biting ability is different in nature. Like snake biting, dog biting, cat biting and even also there are strategies based on mosquito biting. As a female infected anopheles mosquito bites a person, it injects the malaria parasite into him. There are several strategies based on malaria-biting ticks and earned handsome dividends.

It is not yet finalised who is the hero. Whether a strategy is built on the strength of an available campaign or a campaign is being executed at the domination of the strategy. The two best available thinking patterns are conflicting with each other about which is arguably the best. However, the right time to predict it has not come yet.

Though it is an easy pick that, as per the strategy, the campaign should be done, which means the campaign has no say and everything materialises only because of the strategy and thus its ultimate goal does not always excel. When it happens, a civil war erupts between the two, and when such events occur, the only winner is the third party. Thus, to avoid such unfortunate events, both parties embrace each other and act as colleagues where nobody is the boss. If by chance the result exceeds beyond limit and is very near to the desired level, it will be a good sense to give honour to both of them equally. In fact, common sense will do much more than a good sense.

Like common sense, common feeling and common will power, they will always play a vital role in building up a building block. It is like an anatomy of a human body where cells are the basic units of life, and the number of cells put together builds a tissue. Many tissues together form an organ system, and many organ systems together form the human body.

It is a matter of time until a building block is adjudged as the most important underground pillar on which the future multistoried success will stand/be erected.

Thus, if we differentiate, we will only find several building blocks on which a strategy remains standing. A building block is a unit, and therefore it is the basic unit of theory, like as a campaign also follows. The concept is that until you unite the whole structure, the possibilities of macro-error remain. Do not allow these lily-pots to settle carelessly; maybe one day these errors will tear down your whole structure, and nobody will come forward to rescue you.

Whenever you work out your homework for a new course of action, check you are each finished block with a microscope to wipe out any unwanted stupid enemy, and if there is any, immediately destroy them mercilessly. Maybe you are consuming a bit more time to do that, but it will pay you in the future. As it is said, "A stitch in time saves nine". However, do we all make any sense from it? It will be a great hypocrisy if anybody says yes. Because it has never been taken care of.

Why? The answer is very simple. When a large dimension/volume of work has to be done, the amount of time left for re-checking is less. But is it a matter of having less time or less urge? In reality, it is the lack of urge and not time that puts a break on it. It was always there in the guidebook, but always overlooked. Then what kind of rubbish homework did you do? It was seen that hundreds of students in hundreds of math exams were deceived by marks due to this lack of urge for rechecking their answer and thus lost honour marks in the exam.

However, do the students learn their lessons from it? The students learn nothing unless they accept their faults, and it requires guts, but they disguise it by saying they lack time. A student has to learn to control time on their palm with bookish knowledge to excel. Though it seems difficult on paper, in reality, it requires a lot in solving a factorisation, of practice. Another aspect of controlling time is the combination of speed and power in doing a job. If a math student consumes an average time in solving a factorization in 3 minutes, he has to develop both speed and power to solve the same problem in 2.5 minutes. This tiny saving of 30 seconds will put them in a better position to succeed in competitive exams. It also ensures 30% less error to cover, and what an advantage it creates over others! It is arguably the best advantage to be owned and only the stupid shy away from it, thus paying a very high cost in life. Have anybody ever understood that for a mere 30-second lapse, millions of students bankrupted millions of dollars earning and live a miserable fortune? These bankrupters have tried repeatedly to earn the lapse but not a worthy try, proved at last.

A strategy should be divided and subdivided into many building blocks. The more the building blocks, more will be the vigilance, more will be the transparency, and lesser will be the risks. The building blocks may be different in size, but they are still manageable.

There are strategies that have building blocks, each having a constant size and capacity, but it is an injustice to the bearer of the project. Because it sends a wrong signal to the strongest bearer by virtue of an attempt to equalise the excellence he holds over others who are below him. Any such attempt jeopardises the whole effort. Suppose a strategy comprises building blocks having geometrical shapes like a cube, rectangle, rhombus, triangle, etc., which are dissimilar in size and shape. Any attempt to make them similar kills the motivation and the skill of the project bearers.

A right-angle block will give a proper and perfect shape to a structure by its average low profile job, where most of the low-profile project bearers feel happy, while others get bored and feel unhappy. Because the strongest bearer of the project will hate to see their creativity, malfunctioning, and their agony will destroy their skills, leaving them an ordinary person. This will be a great loss of human resources. On the contrary, when a strategy lays down building blocks according to the strength of the implement bearers, it can easily enhance the billion-dollar human resource blank cheque. A recent review on the human resource data projects that Americans yield as high as 10% of the total human resource in comparison to only 3% of Indian origin.

Therefore, this 7% gap is the main culprit that has already gone out of our reach, and thus the selection of an appropriate strategy demands much to balance the ultimate balance sheet. A balance sheet is a final, complete product that causes charges and thus it permanently seals further proceedings. And working into the balance sheet, which has laid duck over a period of time, all souls and hearts of the universe desert it forever.

It is a common practice that success infects success and failure infects failure. Thus, a successful personality always flocks with his counterpart, and interestingly, all unsuccessful personalities flock together.

A strategy is a multicellular body and each of its cells is a building block. In a multicellular body, a group of well-organised cells acts and behaves in a different way to perform different functions from the other cells in the group. Like that, a certain number of building blocks behave and act differently to perform certain functions. Now it is a challenge to equip these building blocks in such a way that they can act as a team, taking and giving support to their co-team members. Each team member also has to understand the job, and the technical know-how has to be well adopted. They have to perform the given task within the time frame and complete it before the time frame. This will earn them an extra standard/height.

Now, how to decide the number of team members and their ability to perform the implementation of the strategy? The choice is always for the best ability, but it is not always available. So there are tactics to develop the underdeveloped to meet certain standards, which are fixed as per the demand. As growth and development an ongoing processes, it pays in the end. A development project is thus nutrition for the underdeveloped.

There is no limit to development, and as such, the strategy will decide at what height is the minimum need. It will be a disaster if the development is very high or less than the expected/requisite standard. It is because development projects always require time and cost. The higher the project, the longer the time and higher the cost. Why is it so?

Can you take your breakfast, lunch, dinner and supper all at a time? You cannot because you have to chew and not swallow your food for proper digestion and to attain nutrition. In addition, the capacity of your stomach is limited. Your stomach demands slow and steady flow, not overflow. Like that, developments demand time and as time is money, it is expensive.

It is a matter of concern how much a strategy can bear. Too much cost yields a pension and too little cost yields a ration. Now what should be an ideal cost ratio?

It varies from field to field, but that does not mean it cannot be measured. It can be measured by detecting intrinsic and extrinsic changes due to investment thrust. Now, how to calculate? Intrinsic property, which is an in-built system, is very difficult to change by injecting money, because its effect does not last long, but there is a demand for change, correctly as a 180-degree change of behavioural pattern for at least a minimum of 180 days as a first phase for entitlement of a ration card at least.

Extrinsic property, which is an external built system, is also very difficult to change by money or power because it changes only when the intrinsic property changes. However, extrinsic property has a plus point, which is that its changes are multiple in nature. Suppose there is a change in the intrinsic system of about 180 degrees, then the minimum extrinsic change that can be expected is 360 degrees. Feel it as a 4-stroke cylinder and thus it is the best car one has to avail it. However, is it very easy to avail? You will see it shortly.

What a game it is, very easy to play, isn't it? However, how to play it and become a clear winner? Before you know how to play, you must know what the game is! Therefore, if you need to learn the game, you must know what these two principal opponents are. Because a game is always played between two parties. So here, the parties are intrinsic and extrinsic. Let us name them as intrinsic gold and extrinsic platinum.

Intrinsic gold consists of eleven players. They are as follows:

1. Lands and buildings.
2. Plants and machinery.
3. R&D.
4. Quality control.
5. HRD
6. Training centres.
7. Environment.

8. Culture.

9. Knowledge.

10. Finance.

11. Balance-sheet.

Extrinsic platinum consists of the following eleven players:

12. Trade unions.

13. Active managers and workers.

14. Working hours lost.

15. Pilfer of money.

16. Failed products.

17. Low packages.

18. Low profile of workers and managers.

19. Centralisation of power.

20. One man authority.

21. Brittle philosophy.

22. Adamancy.

Looking at the player's list, one can easily predict the winner. However, when the game is actually played, it is seen that almost 9 out of 10 times, it is the extrinsic platinum which emerges as the winner. It is shocking, but does it always happen? The only reason is the pressure building attitude and the capacity of extrinsic platinum over intrinsic gold, because of which the intrinsic gold commits easier no of lapses, which decreases their tolerance and abilities. On the other hand, the extrinsic platinum being a weak party has nothing to lose and thus stays aloof from pressure and commits fewer lapses compared to their intrinsic counterparts and becomes the ultimate winner by scoring a platinum goal in the extra time.

Now the question is why they scored goal in the extra time and not in regular time? It is because of the inherent property of both parties. Intrinsic gold is known to be a better performer in regulation time, while extrinsic platinum always prefers anything beyond extra, and thus, when it was offered, they sealed their own goal, depriving their opponent.

It can be said that extrinsic factors are very much opportunistic, while intrinsic factors are egoistic.

The egoistic attitude of the intrinsic factors is not the root cause of their status quo and thus changes very little instead of demand, which may be one of the reasons for their downfall. It is unworthy to say that they are not willing to change, but they are not risking themselves to the right proportion for the fear of the unknown future, which has cost them a lot.

Therefore, a change is must, but a timely change ought to be managed. Because a late change only brings failure and embarrassment, dragging them into failure of uncertainties, when it will apparently reveal an opposite state of thinking, like "what for this change and what is the need to take such a risk?"

Remember, if you do not take risks, everything is at risk. Whatever you owe or retain does not last long unless you add value to it. You may not be aware of how much value you are depreciating every second, which never stops, and unless you feel this smallest spark of depreciation, it keeps multiplying until it becomes a big fireball that burns you into ashes one day.

So always try to add value to your possessions. Do not allow it to rust; instead, you polish the small iron bar of your possession without altering its shape, and that is the simple definition of growth and development and whatever risk is required has to be taken as guaranteed. There is no other choice. You have come to this world to LIVE AND NOT LEAVE.

Now, what is the risk factor the intrinsic club faces? un-warranty:

1. **Land and Building** - One needs a home to stay, not land and building. Because home gives shelter, love, affection, insurance, a feeling of satisfaction, a family that consists of their nearest and dearest ones and their past and present memories. Therefore, if land and building do not change into a home, it is

worthless, and then it becomes a matter of distress and liability one day.

2. **Plants and machinery** - One needs modern plants and machinery to ease the competition and settle in comfort with a prosperous future. If there is no change, the competition will be hard and their future unsettled.

3. **R&D** - Always try to make a change in R&D with new formulations to keep its flag flying and keep it in front as a magnet which catches the attention and inquisitiveness of others.

4. **Quality control** - Try to make an honest qualifying change sincerely in the quality and bring passion into quality service to control others' quality control.

5. **Human resource -** It is said to be the most economical and available resource in countries like India, China, Pakistan and in the African continent. However, it is unfortunate to notice that in spite of a very good job done by the government and private institutions, their utility and conversion effects are not worth mentioning. We are very much lagging behind other industrially advanced countries. In addition, the wastage of such vast potential thus remains a heavy burden to the country. There may be hundreds of reasons, but the most important and urgent cause has remained dormant to date and is asking for a great change, but who cares. There are thousands of HRD in small-scale and

large-scale institutions scattered here and there in the country, but what is the progress rate? Very negligible and embarrassing? It demands a 180-degree change to yield a face-saving index.

6. **Training centre** - Most of the training centres are now becoming commercial centres, where training becomes a commodity to sell, and thus most of them end up run by traders to earn revenue instead of training professionals. These certificates are hence sold to candidates who do not deserve them. Just to maintain the international standard, there are a million miles to go and thus a great change is in the asking for.

7. **Environment** - What is it? It is a place of entertaining virus where the job becomes an entertainment and its entertainers are undoubtedly the motivation. It is a place where job wins absolute freedom from the clutches of slavery and unrest. Such existence of the environment in today's world becomes a dream, and this dream should be converted into reality by accepting challenges.

8. **Culture -** It is a system of picking an age-old belief or trend, where cult means a system of religious belief or trend. Thus, it speaks a volume of gharana, and thus the hardest metal to crack towards renaissance is a great challenge to change.

9. **Knowledge** - It is a system of acknowledging the unknown matter into the cavity of the grey matter of the human brain, and therefore it requires an active involvement and deep concentration, which is also a challenging task.

10. **Finance** - It is an input and it's international ratio is 1:40 which means 1 rupees of input should earn 40 rupees which is a big ask, and thus without a basic change it cannot be achieved.

11. **Balance sheet** - it is a progress report of a business. Just looking into a balance sheet will not give any information regarding how much good or bad work has been done. So, just to keep the momentum of the balance sheet, a great change is required.

Extrinsic players:

1. **Trade unions**- They are like fertile soil, and they more often reap a well-rewarded good harvest. However, never try to get a return from a small reaping, for it will kill the fertility of the soil and make the soil docile within a short period of time. Keeping the return rewarding is therefore a great art that requires extra care to nurse it.

2. **Workers**- They are an important asset, hence complete and perfect utilisation is necessary to counter any challenge, and therefore it is a big task to perform.

3. **Working hours**- As the workforce will never exceed the working hours, it is to be noted that not a single fraction of a second should be lost, and that is why wartime emergency in the working arena is always preferred.

4. **Pilfering of funds**- Though it is very difficult to stop misuse of funds, control over the misuse should be anchored fast.

5. **Flop products**- Never wait too long to dispel flop products from the minds of the people of the corporate team. Instead, try to earn confidence for a new product, and thus it is better to forget the failed product as soon as possible.

6. **Low packages-** Work force with low packages always produce low to very low-quality sets of mind, and thus, nothing like high expectation ever comes from them. So, change the gear and the productivity will certainly improve.

7. **Low profile**- A low profile system produces a low-profile mindset and eventually low productivity, irrespective of a competent manager, as they are human beings emotionally blackmailed. So, a great change is therefore required to correct the system.

8. **Centralisation**- It is a bureaucratic system and thus never returns any good. Decentralisation is necessary for any kind of expected growth, so care must be taken to reverse it.

9. **Authority**- It is a built-up automatic system, which states that responsibility and authority are two prime factors to discharge duty. Nobody can play any infringement if both are well-knit together.

10. **Brittle philosophy**- Without a strong philosophy, a strong buildup is remote, so always accept a strong philosophy to set apart the sharp decline, which is prone to accidental evil.

11. **Adamancy**- Destroying all hard stones can create a crystal clear flexibility to accept reasonable odds and to draw equal importance for everybody.

In reality, extrinsic factors always take the upper hand, and thus intrinsic factors are bogged down and fail to counter any negative pressure from extrinsic factors. As a result, the extrinsic factors govern or dictate the whole proceeding, which is a result of complete failure. What is to be noted here is that these are all manmade deformities in strategy building.

Although there are hundreds of checklists available to prevent the deformity, to date, all those checklists have proved useless, as they are unable to stop it. So newer and newer checklists are adopted and tested, manufactured and tried, with the hope to win over the prevailing situation. It will be a great thing if anything comes out as a permanent cure.

It is not impossible in today's world. All the impossibilities of this world are at stake as they have seen the complete men and they are only concerned about men. Men are their greatest threat to existence or survival. Are they really worried about all men? Absolutely no. They do not bother for all barring a few. Because they know, men are very choosy. Whatever things suit them, they accept and digest, but whatever does not suit them, they simply reject. These groups are not at all their concern. They are concerned for those who are, by and large the different men. These small groups always have the tendency to challenge the awkward situation. They never rest on personal laurels. They consider it a luxury and do not accept. They always run for the volatile essential things, and until the volatility is extracted from the essentials, they do not stop. They have the forensic eye to read under grave/care writing. They do not allow any distraction to poke its nose into their holy war and only settle after the great success is achieved. To them, life is a deal and they are dealing their life only to get to the top. This group of people, however small in number, they are named as Greats/ Legends. When and where any impossible converts into a possible one, these Greats/ Legends play their role. They are the different functionaries responsible for this trick. So, just to avail it, one has to increase one's level toward a greater height to the height of the impossible; this is the bare essential to a great deed.

However, the inputs and outputs prospective balance is wholly credited for the system that plays the sole role in controlling it. Thus, it becomes much regarded nowadays by the people. Actually, the system is a broad-spectrum discipline where the broad spectrum is meant for the wide coverage of disciplines. They are quantity or quality of work, punctuality, honesty, sincerity, and individuality. There are also others too like sanity, austerity, simplicity, tenacity, equity, and maturity.

So much to say that the system is the discipline of all disciplines, the function of all functions. A system is like a busy port, well-connected to the other ports, and is designed to monitor every ship that approaches and leaves the port. It is also well equipped with facilities like off-loading and on-loading. It is often seen that when a system is overburdened, it leads to irreparable damage. This causes a permanent snag. When such snags develop, it should be left to its own destiny. It is a very dangerous phenomenon and thus by all means it should be monitored at the earliest. Even a measure of 30% to 50% snag is not desirable.

Just to avoid this status, it should be put under constant vigil, and before it crosses a permissible limit, which is not more than 40%, a channel should be built, or movements of ships should be restricted well in advance.

It is not economically viable to build a channel; hence, controlling incoming and outgoing ships from the port should be taken into consideration.

A system has to be developed with great care and devotion. Like a human life, a system has four stages- Infancy, Adolescence, young adults and old age, and every stage is vital as all four functions as a team and their reciprocation strengthens the system. The more the reciprocation, more it grows. Reciprocation is a dynamic duct, very common in all stages, resting them in healthy and wealthy. However, the duct changes its total mass from one stage to another. Thus, in all four stages, the duct individual composition is different. It is because of this composition, all four stages perform unique jobs. Power, pressure, elasticity and hardness are different in different stages. Thus, a system could handle the best encounter in the stage 2 & 3, i.e. in the young and adult stage. Its encounter ability gradually diminishes in old age.

Therefore, a system is best built by stage 2 & stage 3 ducts. However, it is proven that a system cannot afford to make without stage 1 & stage 4 ducts. Therefore, it is a general practice that the system invests optimally in the stage 2 and 3and thus receives higher dividend returns in these two stages. On the contrary, stage 1 & stage 4 demand higher investments, but their return is a diminishing one. In one way, it is like depreciation. Therefore, to keep equilibrium and harmony among all four stages of the system enriches its bond.

A bond is a rich heritage of friendship. It shares its weaknesses and strengths, gains and losses with its counterpart, thus the more bonds in the system, the better and more efficient the system is.

The different bonds in a system are not alike, and their unique structure makes each bond unique from one another. As a result, the system is enriched with wide depth, deeply rooted to withstand the whipping challenge.

A system thus always welcomes challenges to check its own base strength. A system should be a wide cylinder to outscore the challenge. If a system's shape is narrow, it may be swept out by the challenge, and thus the system receives a great shock, which is unacceptable.

A system is like a rubber balloon, which receives positive productive as well as negative unproductive air until a permissible limit. Thus, a system should develop the skill to convert the negative, unproductive air into positive, productive air. A system functions almost like the heart of a human being.

If every bond in the system works as a co-partner, it remains strong and invincible, but there is a tendency for the bonds to be over-/less less-reactive, which causes shag in the system. It is a natural phenomenon, and no system can avoid it. Whatever may be the restriction or vigilance, shag will grow eventually, because it is a part of the game.

What is required in this context is just to kill, which causes a snag in its infancy with less venom. The system will run again like before, without much to do.

It should be remembered that it takes years to build a culture, and a system is no doubt a culture that takes time to build. Hence, total dismantling of a system causes unnecessary wastage of time and money.

Time and money are the two hottest resources of all. All the systems created, therefore, have to deal with two. How to deal with them and with what great care to be enforced to maximise their utilities are the biggest questions that remain unanswered.

In a mission to earth the unearth, the science of systems took birth in the past. Today's science and technology both incorporated into every system as fuel to get the best mileage.

Everywhere, there is talk of it, and no doubt it is the chicken soup of this day and at night. Everyone wants to get as close as possible to it. Because the finest picture is yet to develop from the darkroom.

Thus, what was yesterday's program is no doubt today's program, and the future will be the same, unless the complete behavioural patterns of time and money can be well visualised.

It is a saying that "Time is money", but saying "Money is time" has not been achieved yet. It was not achieved because both things are not exchangeable as vice versa. The reason is that money is a tangible good, but time is intangible. Both things vary from each other by a mile. Therefore, there is a battle between distance and power.

We must win the battle by establishing their relationship between. It is feasible in today's thinking. When we can establish a relationship with the planet

Mars, our trial-and-error effort to establish a time and money relationship is not far behind.

Let us see what the algebraic equation states.

1. Time=Money.

Then it should be

1. Money inversely proportional to Time (has to be proved).

We can also discuss the two equations as such:

1. Money is time is an intangible equation
2. Money is directly proportional to Time is a tangible equation.

In business, the first equation is a combination of **Strategy and Action plan**. The second equation is a **dividend ratio**.

Alternatively, the first equation is an **investment**. The second equation is a **profit/loss quantity.**

How is a relationship carried in life? A relationship materialises on the strength of time and money. It takes time for a relationship to develop truly and permanently by trial trial-and-error method. On the contrary, a false and temporary relationship grows when time is scarce.

Let us consider money. When money is used as a sponsor to build a relationship, the more the money is involved, the greater the vacuum created in the relationship. In this context, money is the culprit and the curse.

However, when money plays the role of a censor in the creation of a relationship, the degree of vacuum in the relationship is almost nil. In this context, money is the clear winner and a great blessing.

Let us apply both these principles in business from individual ones. What will be the outcome? Let us call it as **ACID TEST.**

In business, where money is a big sponsor, it attains sharp peaks and troughs in graphical data due to immature relationships.

However, in business, where relationship or time is a sponsor, attains optimum peaks and troughs in graphical data due to a mature relationship.

So, what we have seen is the importance of relationship, which is a maker of **ONE SWEET SMILE, COSTING 1 MILLION DOLLARS.**

The fundamental thing is to prepare a healthy relationship between time and money. A process will invariably help everybody individually or in a group. Thus, there is a need to know **"TIME MANAGEMENT"** and **"MONEY MANAGEMENT."**

All the leading national and international B schools are now invading these two unknown hidden treasures, which is without a doubt an experimental learning process. The more we try to experiment with both, the more and more new data and equations will come out.

What is now available and what is still in the dark are the two vital aspects, disturbing a lot because of the marked gap, i.e. **AVAILABILITY** vs. **REALITY.**

The latest available knowledge about time management left us all in a state of debate because there is no such breakthrough which can extract more than 10% to 15% of the total human resource in the world.

However, we know that all the greats could easily achieve as many as 40% of their total human resource long before. Definitely, there is something which is eluding us repeatedly.

What is there with the greats like Swami Vivekananda and Rishi Arobindo, which is lacking in today? Let the top identity of an international B school of today's so-called greats answer the question.

Couldn't anybody on this earth ever be able to challenge Swami Vivekananda by generating a better and more efficient human resource development power? It is not possible. It is not at all, because no classroom can teach the excellence of human resource development. To master a human resource, one has to perceive, and no bookish knowledge will ever be available anytime, anywhere on this earth, which is almost certain.

However, it is necessary, and you have to deliver the best for your own identity. So, what do you have to do? You have to do the best thing. Sit and think about time management. What is it? How do you manage the time? Simple solution, which is of today's logic- just to run and run.

Get up in the morning by running, take your bath by running, have your breakfast by running, do your homework by running and so on. You will be able to manage your time. Do the greats ever manage their time this way? No and never. After a few days of running, you will not only feel uncomfortable but will certainly develop the compulsion to quit. Because you are against the odds. You will say that if you continue, you might get lost.

The prime objective of time management is to manage you and not time. Because you are not worthy of managing time. You may be a lord, but not God. God has given you the best gift of 24 hours. So do not try to dig a hole into it. Also, never try to underplay or overplay your role. It will be of no use. However, try to play your master role.

If you are an employee in a bank and your job is to accept money from your customers from 10 A.M. to 2 P.M., apart from your fingers, you have no outside help. Your customers are more against the normal status quo. However, you have only 4 hours to finish the job, and that too with a big smile on your face. What will you do to manage time?

1. You can complain with your affiliated union to rescue you.
2. You may ask to open an additional counter to ease pressure.
3. You may ask for a computer.

Suppose none of the above-mentioned options is available to you. Then how will you manage? This is your own problem. You are well paid to do it. Will you manage your own problem, or will you quit? You have decided it for yourself.

If you are an intelligent and knowledgeable person, you will try to readjust your position by changing your vision. Your vision is your own eternal help, which never deserts you. Your vision power will elevate your skill to excel.

Let it not be theoretical but a practical one.

1. The first approach should be to see yourself among the customers who come to you every day.
2. The sales will be closed if you see they bought on.
3. Your next step is to buy the customer vision.

By attempting the above three steps, you will not only ensure an earlier position up a bit, but you will also be able to achieve success in settling the whole issue. By doing this, one day you will earn the masterpiece of the art of management.

How will you do it? First approach: Your bank customers are many in number. However, they can be easily categorised into different groups. This can be done as follows:

1. Very important and regular customers, depositing heavy amounts every day in cash. They always ask for a bank'sfavour, i.e. overdraft. Amount of loan. They should be your last preference.
2. Very important and regular customer depositing heavy cash every day but never asks for any kind of favour. They should be your first preference.
3. Important but regular customers who deposit large amounts of cash in intervals but always ask for the bank's favour. Make them your first preference.
4. Less important but regular customers. Deposits small cash regularly but never asks for any favour from the bank. Make them your first preference.

Let us see how you will be able to sell to all of them:

a) Welcome the most valued customer with a big smile and put questions asking them questions about their whereabouts.

Telling them how important they are to you and the bank.

Make the customer aware that he is a different one, as such, he has no business in queuing up and convince him to meet you at zero hours, but never forget to convey that the mission of today's visit will be taken care of.

b) Wish the most valued permanent customer with a long smile and do not ask anything, but act in such a way that the customer gets a feeling of warmth and allows it to be imprinted on their minds for quite some time.

You can also ignore all the petty wrong entries if the customer on his cheque / account slip posted it and gets it corrected by the customer at your kind solicitation.

You can also ask for extra service to be rendered other than banking rituals.

c) Welcome the valued customer and forget to give him a favour available in your box until the customer changes his irregular visits to the bank.

At the time of rendering bank service to this group of customers, allow the customer to do some side talk and get information about the favour the customer truly received from competitors.

If feasible, book the customer permanently on the spot, for he may be your good investment in the future.

d) This group of customers never changes their habits, nor has the decency to think about it. On the contrary, they wish to receive a welcome and a good reception every time they invade. Show your cool to them, but offer service if required.

Never allow them to stay extra than the requisite time and sort out their problem on a war footing.

If possible, do not allow them to talk, even with the most important customers.

Customers are so large, yet it looks like a small matchbox for you. Let it be a uniform stick, powered with igniting capacity, finely knitted. Store them all the time in a safe; otherwise, it is very dangerous. While they are always stored, try to breed them with a mood to fulfil your demands. It is undoubtedly a skill that only a magician possesses. **Mesmerising skills**.

To achieve such a skill, you have to raise yourself to the level of a magician. All the great salespeople of the past and present, thus, are able magicians and truly a different class of people.

All customers remain satisfied as long as they feel they are beneficiaries of the expenditure. Thus, to be a beneficiary is a right of the customer, and as long as it is sustainable, it is a will for you. It is true that a customer signs a will for you unknowingly. Knowledgeably, a customer is always a loser, but it is the architect of a salesperson who engineered the feeling of beneficiaries in the mind of the customer.

Engineering such a feeling in the customer's mind is an uphill task. Yes, it is an uphill task for an average person, but a salesperson converts it to a downhill task. He just rolls the customer down from up, never lifts the customer from down. Because lifting a customer is a hard task, a salesperson tries to avoid it intelligently. Let the customer run to earn comfort and money. However, let the customer feel that he earns the comfort with his money. In real life, no customer could achieve this objective. It is because most customers do not know the knowhow to acquire true comfort.

Only a salesperson knows it, and after selling the know - how to the customer, the salesperson makes the customer a beneficiary. It is an endless game because comforts are changing in nature around the clock. It is very difficult to keep up with the fast-paced status of comfort. If an intelligent or alert customer tries hard to concentrate on the change, his concentration on money earning will be disturbed and will change from customer to salesperson.

Yes, then a customer becomes a salesperson and certainly destroys his old identity, an identity will earlier made him satisfied as a customer because a position of a customer is always higher than a salesperson. This thought will burn him.

Customer always feels high when they are awarded these types of positions, and he who awards the position to the customer is a clever one and no doubt, he is a champion salesperson. Because such an award is rendered to a customer, it always rewards a salesperson's image. Hence, all this time, when a customer was awarded, say one rupee, the customer rewarded the salesperson with not less than fifty rupees unknowingly.

Everywhere there is a tendency to pickpocket the customer by treating him as a God. This is nothing but a wicked trick to infringe on a customer. Infringement on a customer is a tricky art that remains dormant. Yet the customer never notices it. A customer's mind is always full of risk and doubt created by the salesperson. The creative agents are the art of success over a customer.

In reality, it is like a got-up game. The salesperson knows the outcome of the game well in advance. Still, he plays a role, which often never seems to be vague in the customer's eye. Most of successful salesperson often has the power to convert negative prospects into positive ones.

This kind of trick is a mesmerising act to cheat a customer. Because a salesperson knows that unless the customer's mind and heart are very confused, he cannot achieve his objective. So a salesperson always tries to raise doubts and risks in the mind of his customer constantly, until the customer completely bestows his decision-making power in the hands of the salesperson.

It is well understood that all the customers are bad swimmers. By bad swimmers, it means a person who knows how to swim but never practices enough to be a good swimmer. A salesperson is a top-class Olympic gold medalist in swimming. There are no such strokes in swimming that he cannot perform. Moreover, he develops the art of sailing smoothly over the untidy and noisy waves around the clock.

By raising risks and doubts in the mind of the customer, he makes a great profit. He is thus able to convert the situation intelligently. By raising more doubts and risks, he wants to bury the customer under such a turmoil situation that inevitably makes the customer perplexed, and as such, the customer ends up gambling for everything asked for by the salesperson. In addition, whenever the customer gambles, the salesperson always wins the jackpot. Because all the trump cards are intentionally hidden by him. Unfortunately, the customer is not a professional gambler. Hence, the salesperson keeps the customer tied to him by transferring a fraction of the profit he made, which keeps the customer satisfied, happy and trapped. In the meantime, the salesperson keeps getting richer.

However, Time is the greatest opposite force always playing a great role to reduce the degree of hostage. Thus, a clever salesperson will play his role not only to retain his old customers but also to create new ones. If a salesperson fails to do that, he will eventually lose the battle in the market operation. Nevertheless, there is a high risk involved in retaining old customers because it always backfires.

It backfires because keeping an old customer hostage for too long is a matter of high risk and can lead to huge loss for a salesperson. Both these two factors are of prime input used by a salesperson to build themselves up and to act in a mature kind of way. It is therefore an important scale to be accurately accounted against the velocity of the outputs. An old customer, therefore, remains hostage as long as possible, but its credibility is always in doubt.

As time is the greatest healer since its discovery, an old customer develops antibodies to engulf the wear and tear of hostage law. In quest of freedom, this antibody gradually spreads its division of cells to create antibodies, and with time, it becomes so imprudent that to retain an old customer hostage becomes a heavy burden and punishment for a salesperson. However, it is not impossible to retain him long by exercising unprofitable inputs, which the old customer demands, but it is a big cost, and no salesperson wants to drain his inputs and labour. Therefore, it is better to let the old customer go.

Therefore, what we have seen here is that it is not possible to spread a business network without creating new customers. Thus, when old customers at some point leave a salesperson's voyage, he has to fill the ship by creating new ones. Now, what is the limit of such at some point? Generally, to gauge this exact time always confuses and worry. However, I suggest that retaining an old customer for more or less than 5 years is against the salesperson's hostage law.

A salesperson's hostage law is always in favour of a customer who is delivering their faith and trusts in a brand for at least 5 years. Less than 5 years means the customer is immature and judged the brand by chance and not by choice. The reason is very simple and very complex for a salesperson. When a salesperson tries to create a customer by dishonest means, he has to pay for it in the end. It is, therefore, a wrong methodology, an immature one, and an irresponsible salesperson can only venture it. Whatever the cost of creating such a half-headed customer may cost, it is not at all recoverable, and the extent of the loss causes the salesperson to lose his identity and credibility.

Thus, it is welcomed that if a customer is awaited and whatever the structure of the cost, the customer should be retained for at least 5 years and not more than that. An honest salesperson always achieves this objective squarely. What a salesperson has to practice and earn from the customer should be done within the first 5 years. Because if he makes a mistake of acting too fast, he will lose the customer before the stipulated time and thus will earn a big duck, and by acting too slow, he will also sacrifice his earnings by a big margin as it will allow the customer to overeat the salesperson's strategy in earning profit. Therefore, in dealing with this retaining customer, one should neither act too fast nor act too slow.

It is a continuous process and is easily comparable with the in-built human cell system. A cell in the human body divides by mitosis and matures with an urge to create newer, young cells to replace the old and the dead. Thus, wear and tear of a cell is a normal phenomenon. Like the cell, the customer also undergoes wear and tear and eventually gets old. Thus, to replace the old customer with a young one, a salesperson always remains on the hunt to create a new one, and whoever is more potent in new and young customers wins the distinction of being a very good salesperson.

Therefore, the two most important tasks of a salesperson are to retain old customers and to create new and young customers in a way that keeps the system healthy and strong. In this pursuit, a salesperson ends up virtually knocking on every prospective customer.

Most of the prospective customers remain dormant to a salesperson, and it is his skill to give light and oxygen enough to convert a dormant bud into a colourful blooming flower. A successful salesperson always lends his gifting hand forward and hides his receiving hand. It is a skill which a salesperson develops by assessing the situation.

It is a fact that a potential customer always avoids a salesperson for fear of being hijacked. Hencc, a salesperson has to prove their worth by citing the right concern to their customer. When a perfect salesperson can create concern in the mind of the customer for which he does not have the right solution, the customer will seek his help to get out of the situation. Thus, the customer willingly hands himself over to the salesperson out and out without knowing its real cost. Now a salesperson's job is to elaborate on the real cost the customer has to incur without showing any kind of mercy. Therefore, a salesperson ends up dictating the terms and conditions at their will to get the maximum mileage. As soon as the customer has agreed, the deal should be completed without any further delay. Any delay in sealing the deal will backfire, and the whole effort might go in vain.

Hijacking and taking hostage of a customer's will is of utmost need for a salesperson, without making the customer aware of it. A salesperson can reveal it only after completing his business with his customer before the permissible limit expires. Because even the world's top salesperson will admit that it is impossible to keep a customer satisfied beyond a certain point.

It is therefore imperative that the salesperson does not lose the customer and does everything possible to make the customer feel happy. Because if the customer comes to know about the reality, he may feel cheated and sad, this can be considered a defeat for the salesperson. Both the salesperson and the customer should always enjoy the rat race and feel good for making the system active and warm.

The whole marketing devices are allocated to engineer the strong affinity bond between the customer and the media person, i.e. the salesperson. A salesperson being the driver of the bond voyage should always remain positive, and under no circumstances should they allow any doubt to resurface that could change the direction of the motivation. The affinity bond always remains stable as long as the opposite forces remain uniform. It does not mean that the affinity bond cannot withstand any force. It is, and to the degree that high force is applied to it cannot be jeopardised for a certain period.

A relation of affinity bond is rechargeable. However, a fresh affinity bond works better than a rechargeable one. It is, therefore, noteworthy to flesh out the maximum in that period. There is no limit to maximisation.

It is unfair to think that if a certain customer is used from toe to head, the salesperson will lose him in no time. Maybe that customer can only be used once, and if that is the case, then it is better to use him to the maximum. If a salesperson fails to do it, he will be throwing this opportunity to his competitor.

Yes, imagination and emotion are the two most strong and weakest spots of a salesperson. Spotless imagination and mature emotion are thus the two vital factors that separate a skilled salesperson from an unskilled one. A skilled salesperson creates hunger in the mindset of his customer by his spotless imagination and mature emotions, while an unskilled one destroys it.

Thus, it is to be decided about how much a skilled salesperson should stretch at a certain time to touch the mental set-up of the customer and then to hijack the whole system. There is no place for partial business. To own the complete mental set-up of the customer is a special skill of an excellent salesperson. They are world-class who vetoes their customer's mental set-up to a total standstill.

These classes of salesperson can use their customer more than the other groups, but the frequency of action should be faster than the others. Because it is very difficult to keep the total blockade for a long time. On the other hand, a salesperson can achieve their objective by walking when there is no duration limit. The tricks may differ, but the objectives are achieved with a greater degree of success.

Often, a salesperson tries to find a solution to the customer's financial potential instead of their mental potential. This is a big mistake. Whatever may be the financial power of a customer, unless he sells his mental set-up to the salesperson, his financial potential is of little value.

It is a matter of the salesperson's self-interest that prevents him from U-turn. However, a gradual turn is necessary for his own survival. Though a sudden turn like a U-turn always produces doubt in the mind of his customers, which is harmful, it is necessary to keep a healthy rapport between them and vice versa.

Often, a salesperson possesses a great wealth of mind and soul, which drives him near to success faster than other professionals are trying to gain. The reason is very simple. When other professionals are trying to gain materialistic things, the salesperson in question is eyeing gains, which cannot be measured on materialistic grounds.

An immaterialist gain will never be lost once achieved. This is in contrast to materialistic gains, which are temporary.

Trust, goodwill, brand image, logo, confidence and image all belong to the immaterialist wealth, which is very hard to achieve, and are time-consuming. However, once it is achieved, it is permanent. However, earning, money and profit are materialistic gains and are temporary.

This is the way of thinking of a salesperson. A salesperson, therefore, will never risk his immaterial gain for materialistic gain, however big the gain looks. On the contrary, a smart salesperson will accept a loss for the time being to double his immaterial gains.

A salesperson will never die if his immaterial wealth is well kept. It is his only investment to keep himself alive and active. It is said that a noble salesperson is better felt in his absence. His absence fetches him more adoration and attachment. Many times, a pitch of a gap evolves higher obligation. It is often seen that the motivation of obligation of a wonderful customer draws him towards the salesperson.

Like Newton's third law of motion, not only does the salesperson attack a customer, but the customer also attacks the salesperson. The attacking power is so irresistible that it dislodges the customer and makes him a permanent traveller. Therefore, a customer who was earlier static becomes dynamic at the quest of the salesperson's salesmanship craft, and no doubt, his salesmanship craft is his only possession of immaterial values.

As a business has to grow for its own survival, the immaterial values also need to grow for its own longevity, and thus repeatedly, immaterial values have to be redressed for a new launch. It is beyond any doubt that when things become old, they lose their charm. To make it and keep it attractive, it has to be reformulated with new and young alternative looks that will not only enhance its glory but also make it a smart competitor to gain the top ladder.

Therefore, what we have learnt is that, like a material object, an immaterial object also needs further investments to grow and gain.

Some situations arise when everything goes wrong-planning, implementation of the strategy. In addition, when that happens, the world's best-experienced award-winning theories and rigid control look helpless and painstaking. What should one do or how should one react in such particular situations? In one way, when not all worthy lethal weapons can win you the battle, are hit back by a standstill, and lose the battle, does everything get lost? A true general always acknowledges defeat sportingly by apprising the opponent, which not only earns self-respect but also minimises the risk of mental upset.

A brave general in his career span has to fight numerous battles. Therefore, losses and wins should not be taken seriously, says the textbook. However, reviewing a loss or a win must be done for safety measures. A safety measure is to ensure that errors are not repeated by taking lessons from it, which is very important.

It is said that learning lessons from others' mistakes is more important and beneficial than learning lessons from one's own mistakes. In today's scenario, clever man scores more points and improve their tally by negotiating others' mistakes skillfully, which not only saves time but also money. Both are of great importance in a person's life. However, as they say, "Time is money," one must be very strict about time and should understand the limitation of time and thus proper utilisation of time brings confidence and self-esteem.

One must rest assured that though money is a habitual betrayer but time is never to be. Time is always a true obedient pupil to its great master. Both are the trump cards of life, but of opposite identity.

Unlike money, time is the only true friend of life if no mistakes are considered. However, if considered, both are the two real strong legs to haunt the unaccounted uncertainties of life. Therefore, one should not be afraid of mistakes. On the contrary, one should adore them. Because only through it can one gain true lessons. However, it is dangerous to always depend upon one's own mistakes to learn the lessons. Because it takes away precious time in life. It is therefore speculated that one must try to gain more lessons from others' mistakes and no doubt, it is the best way to groom oneself.

One might be compelled to think that mistakes mean killing or destroying valuable time. Yes, it is, that is the reason that mistakes should never be repeated, as it is demotivating. Many great men of the past have learnt lessons from their own mistakes and therefore, one should not shy away from it. Never try to shy away from your mistakes. Because if mistakes are not corrected, they will multiply and at last the whole system will be a wholesome burden of errors that ends up destroying the system eventually.

Is anything a possibility without a certain degree of mistakes? The answer is a big NO. However, those mistakes should be corrected so that they are never repeated. Correcting mistakes requires a great deal of accuracy and effectiveness. It requires the highest degree of competency and a great desire for assertiveness and awareness. A stitch in time saves nine. A person who saves their valuable time by not stitching nine times is nine times more potential than their counterparts.

Complete attention to correcting mistakes saves a huge amount of time and reduces loss. Whatever the urgency, any mistake should never be kept alive. Because a mistake is like bacteria, it will invade our system very slowly by multiplying itself. Till the time it becomes difficult to distinguish it and becomes a part of the system. Thus, leaving a mistake unattended is a bad habit.

Bad habits are bad, but worse is to leave them unattended. Habits, good or bad, are generally built on gene structures. Human beings do not have any control over them. Then what is the answer? The answer is that only good habits can control the bad ones. Good habits are like luminous objects, such as stars. The sun is a star. When the sun shines, it generates billions of watts of light energy. On the contrary, by dint of this most powerful light energy, the sun can hide its shortcomings like black spots, which can be considered its bad habits.

On the other hand, the sun has its limitations, like many other materials in this universe. The sun also possesses many harmful gases which are not only harmful but also destructive, but who cares? Has anybody ever complained? Why is it so? It is because everybody believes that the sun is a fabulous object and its level is as high as God's. In ancient times, people used to worship the sun, and even today, this concept is relevant. That is why people are less interested in finding out the sun's fault even though the sun has many shortfalls and weaknesses. However, as the mind's is already filled with a good qualitative image of the sun, it will never agree to pour any factual bad image of the sun. The reason is never urged but generally agreed upon. It is a process of covering the weakness of a time-tested and accepted materialistic thing. Although there is no shortage of clever man who have questioned the integrity of the sun repeatedly, most believe them as mad and attribute their act to a sort of madness. It is an unbreakable custom and notion still going on strongly, which has no real base at all. That is how all the good things in our universe cover up their bad show. People all over the world as MYTH. Thus, accept it.

However, it has been proven many a times that an overused myth gradually loses its acceptability and accountability like a sharp edge, which gets blunt due to overuse. Therefore, the change in custom and belief may be after a few millennia, do not matter. It ought to change, and the day it will change, people will be thrilled to acknowledge the discovery.

In the pursuit of discoveries, the greatest minds are working hard and at last, we came to know that our nearest neighbour, the moon, which appears to be spotless, is actually not as it appears. Like all other materialistic things, the moon has its own roughs and troughs, the good and the bad. At first, when the black spots on the moon were noticed, we were reluctant to believe it. How can it be? However, after a long debate and the acquisition of scientific data and pictures released by space agencies, we are forced to believe the reality. However, our mindset is such that unless we see it ourselves, we do not believe it. Hence, the black spot on the moon, though very tiny, left the moon in an earthly place, where everybody and everything ought to be a sum of the mixed images, the good and the bad.

We are thus able to find out easily the good and the bad, if only we remain vigilant, alert and active, whatever things they are. Therefore, theoretically, a law governs all the earthly things are the total of plus and minuses, the positives and the negatives. Based on these hard facts, science gears up its explanation to explore the unexplored.

It is a fact that human beings, geniuses or average, are bound to adhere to certain laws and principles, and as such, no genius is absolutely free from errors and shortcomings. However, a genius never exposes his weakness by sheer magical intellectual equity, which the average person lacks. An average person can never rise up to the occasion and therefore remains underperformed, and most of their inner talent remains lost in dormancy.

It is true that millions of average people possess good talents, but are unable to develop it due to a lack of confidence and a positive attitude. Their precious possessions, which had tremendous market value, stayed hidden in the dark for many years and are lost forever. It is a tragedy that one day it becomes a posture. These draining out of millions of latent talents serve whom? Surely, these do not serve humankind. On the contrary, this is a great waste, but who cares? A little care would have been a reversed picture, and undoubtedly, the whole of humankind would have benefited from it.

However, who will lend his or her time to the petty things? It is a fashion nowadays to oil the oil mills, and this feels a satisfaction. This is a changing scenario everywhere, and every person who cannot find his or her true path of success gets humiliated. That is why a very tough and sincere conviction has to be taken to never allow them to stay in the wastebasket. On the contrary, they should be honoured all over the world. Because they have to show their mettle. Therefore, it is a challenge for the whole lot to come out with excellence. Once it is achieved, history will write a new chapter, and the outsiders will get a newborn baby in age and care.

It is a matter of great privilege for anyone to be at the top. No doubt when the almighty created his creations, he always blessed it to become the very best. There are many fields and faculties, so it is not as if millions of people are interested in becoming the very best. It is not true. It may appear that there are numerous contestants, but in reality, their number is quite less. Let us carry out an easy experiment. In class X, there are two sections, each comprising 60 students. Therefore, in total, there are 120 students. Do you think that all the 120 students are eyeing to become the topper in the class? The answer is **NO**. At the very best, only around 10% of the total students are in the race to become the topper.

Yes, the most intelligent and the potential candidate are looking at the small group of contestants only. They measure their strength and weaknesses too. It requires great skill to undertake the deeds, but as they are serious about being the very best, they never stop gathering information about that small group of contestants, which helps them in measuring the strengths and weaknesses of their competitors from all directions. Gaining every bit of resourceful information about their competitors helps them to dodge past them in the competition easily. Therefore, it becomes mandatory to know the closest fist of competitors before they are closed.

Never let anyone recognise you as one of the competitors until the D-day come. Let them recognise you only on D-day when it is too late to make any last-minute changes to their desired skill and thoughts. Because time is very short. Do not be nervous. Because it is an opposite climax for you, as time is icy and long for you. Enjoy the time and temperature of your good luck.

The most important aspect of a competitor is to compete and not to complete the process in a hurry. It is because a competitor can only start it, and the closing time better stays with the other person who controls it. So why is there a hurry? It is not required at all. The pace will automatically accelerate, and a time will come when it will ignite all its heat, which is the in-built system of the process.

The only thing required is a competitive mindset to win the competition and nothing more. However, this is easily ignored by most of the competitors, and therefore, trying to do something extra leads them to their downfall because it was never practised before. So why carry out such an experiment it such a critical hour? It is a matter of over-enthusiasm and overactivity. However, it is incorrect. Most people are punished by incorrect methods. Lie straight, close both eyes, and visualise all wonderful powers of nature to spread over your whole body and bathe over a period of time, which will help the mind and the brain will easily connect the dots to counter any obstacles. This will help in smooth sailing.

Most of the time, it is observed that most of the contestants unnecessarily become highly charged when they are in a state of over-boiling the egg. This not only degrades the quality and the nutritive value but also tastes bad. The same things happen with the answer sheets of the contestants. A normal answer sheet looks different from a tampered answer sheet in many ways. They are qualitatively superior and less error-prone, which is a hallmark of the natural activities of the students.

Back-to-back questioning is better than answering. It is a better style of any stage answering in a high-tech system. Everyone expects a different methodology to do a thing other than the usual way of doing it. It is not very difficult but has to be well performed by practising the method. In today's highly competitive field, everyone knows the answer and the theory. However, in the real field, the only thing that matters is how well it is implemented or executed. In every field, therefore, it becomes almost essential to modernise the old script. It not only rejuvenates but also energises. When in a practical development, parties are energised, the convictions become mature and therefore, well-conceived to bear fruit.

In today's world, business virtually depends on a single theory: "How to convince a customer? How fast and how long?" Seconds, minutes, hours, days, months and years are nothing but arithmetic figures. However, in business, it is money. When a potential business starts, it starts with zero, but it starts replacing the zero with figures down the line very fast.

Really, adding pace is the very best way to celebrate a business's growth over time. A growing business always speaks that it is on the right path. Therefore, it can be maintained only by the healthy support of the customers. However, what type of customers are required for this? Dedicated? Wholehearted? Bonded? The answer is NO. Madness and only madness. Most of the successful corporate giants, therefore, endlessly try to hunt for more and more mad customers. However, who are those mad customers? In addition, how are they conceived? They come from all levels of our society, having different purchasing power but possessing a hostile mindset of thinking. This hostility shapes the thinking into a mature one and leads to their interpretation. Is it not surprising that a mad customer perceives something very funny? It may be a chewing gum or a chocolate bar. Fascination, inclination, adoption, emotion, conviction, association and obligation, all clubbed together, make up the mindset of the mad customer. It is a mindset that never changes, and even if it changes, it changes for more saturation and concentration. Sometimes it may change for a firm look and external orientation.

To get an honest answer for the perfect definition of a mad customer often seems contradictory. Because it changes and keeps on changing over the years.

Whatever the changes going on, the head remains unchanged. It is the tail, which is changing like the roots of a banyan tree. The roots of a banyan tree are virtually engraved deep inside the soil in a zigzag manner and remain invisible from above. Similarly, a mad customer's zigzag tail often remains unmarked. Why is it very difficult to uproot it? Because once a customer grasps a certain brand, he absorbs it and remains absorbed with the brand for a long time.

That is the only reason the world's top business companies remain heavily embroiled in the mad customer. Most of the world's top companies are thus doing research to acquire new skills to mesmerise their customers. Note the mad customer's lifelong requisition with a brand such as "COLGATE". With the expansion of the brand and regular consumption of the product, the mad customer continues to pay heavy revenues to the company. Therefore, it is the prime objective for any company to look for such customers.

It is a matter of confirmation that mad customers normally inject the brand name into their blood. They feel satisfied and rejuvenated whenever they use their dream brand. Here lies the trick. Most of the companies that are looking for short-term benefits degrade the quality of their product and therefore end up cheating their customers. They think that their customers are drowsy and uncurious. They should understand that to retain their loyal customers, they need to maintain a higher profile by continuously upgrading their facilities and the quality of their products. However, they think it is useless to do this extra work for their customers, who they think are non-volatile and will stick to the brand no matter what. On the contrary, they offer extra to catch new customers, which they always need to keep up the balance of customer profiles. However, hurting the belief of a permanent customer is a sin and a great crime. Maybe for extra benefits or merely a casual approach, these kinds of policies are adopted, which do not give them any long-term benefits. Whatever extra profits these companies earn are drained out as easily earned money always gets misplaced and vanishes into the air without contributing anything to the real needs of the companies.

Any business decision taken should help organisation in getting its every output to be rolled automatically without disruption. Therefore, every decision-making has to be pinpoint and meticulously done to save time and hard-earned money. In a way of this methodological system, it is thus understood that only the already proven successful strategy is adopted. Most of the companies are not willing to bear the extra cost of experimenting with a new policy. Therefore, most of the R&D sector of the average performing companies is forced to adopt strategies borrowed from others to survive. It is a negative approach, which disables a company in the long run. Because they have to face the tremendous pressure of competition throughout their functioning. In addition, these companies fail to dominate the market as their market share always remains less than what is required to become a decision-making strong company.

However, even an average-performing company should have its own style of living like the different species living on this planet. The most important thing is to create an infrastructure that will safeguard the functioning of the company. Unless it is done, the company will never run smoothly. Any kind of air gapping in the system will be held responsible for the weak link that will eventually break the rhythm of the functioning. Therefore, it is of utmost importance that the rhythmic life of functioning is maintained, as it not only saves costs but also reduces errors.

Though most of the modern business manufacturing houses have the luxury of R&D centres, but how much they render good to the houses is a matter of real concern. It is because R&D people always talk half-baked truth, and their version is contradictory. Half-baked truth means half chances, i.e. 50-50. This results in dismal outputs irrespective of good investments into the inputs, which is of great concern. It is noted that there remains very little time for trials of the product. Because some new products require more than a normal period, the results of the trial are not uniform across all the places where the trial is conducted.

On the other hand, a short-term trial may backfire in the future and almost knock out the product. It is therefore a custom that at all times, the specimen of the product has to be changed, validating its past errors. It is a safeguard policy, but not the most advanced policy. Because most of the previous owners may complain about the problem with the product and the changing look of the product. A customer always becomes proud by having the latest model, which should at least last for 3-5 years. However, today's policy system is against this. It is changing its specimen every day, making the owner sad and helpless. Therefore, all the companies should look into the matter so as to prevent hurting their customers. Because if the customer is hurt, he will never recommend the product to his near and dear ones.

Unfortunately, these business houses try to rule the customer's head and toe, making the customer deaf and dumb and thereby, silently takes away their hard-earned penny. One side of this motivation of the business houses got the damage so vehemently that they had to re-establish/ re-start the relationship in a volatile atmosphere.

A healthy relationship has an optimal transactional power that has to be maintained irrespective of all odds. However, sometimes, very delicate and difficult situations prevail, when all kinds of ethics are bruised, which compels the business houses to burn down the customer relationship. However, it should never be continued for a long time because, if it crosses the permissible limit, it breaches the entire path.

It is very dangerous to recon that losing a customer often takes a fraction of a second, but creating a customer may take months, even years. Therefore, it is a great tragedy on the part of the business house to take the wrong route.

A growing business house never practices the attitude to destroy its own building blocks, unless it starts behaving like a rabid dog. A rabid dog never hesitates to bite its master. For a rabid dog, it is normal to bite anything and anyone that comes in its way until it is put down.

Therefore, what a mischievous deed by a company which does not care to keep alive its own created paths. Nursing each category of customer is the prime need of a company to survive in all competitions. Actually, a competition means owning a certain chunk of customers from others. Therefore, there is a tug of war between the different competitors. In addition, the tug of war is to win over the customer. However, a customer never wants to be pulled into the tug of war. A customer feels pain and is bothered when they are treated as that silly rope. However, there is no doubt that the company created them or faced them or customers to become identical state. Ask a single customer if they really feel proud or if they are comfortable with it. The majority will provide you with a negative answer. Still unknowingly, they become a part of the opera and most of them contribute to the business more than 100%. The magic card played by the companies makes the customer spellbound and takes away their power of reasoning. On the contrary, the customer becomes a dummy in the hands of the company. In modern marketing theory, most of the customers actually contribute to being played by the company. What a helpless situation it is for any customer to be in!

"Professionalism and Benchmark"

The concept behind the whole narrative is to bring *professionalism* to every sector governed by its individuals/ professionals. To attain a *benchmark*, which might serve as a yardstick to judge or test a program's running speed, power and reliability. This is a process to identify and adopt best practices that can improve one's own performance and what should be a hallmark of competence, probity, steadiness, thoroughness, acumen, dedication, sophistication and willingness.

"Figure of Poor Judgement"

Because I don't like to see anybody be a victim of poor judgment in his life, like *Edward John Smith*, the captain of the unsinkable ship TITANIC in 1912.

Inspiration

A whopping $ 670,000 annual salary at the age of only 26 in 1916 made him the wealthiest person in the world, when his childhood in London was one of poverty and hardship. His father abandoned him in childhood, and his mother struggled financially, who said, "***Nothing is permanent in this wicked world, not even our troubles.***" He also said, "***I always like walking in the rain, because no one can see me crying.***"

When Albert Einstein met him in 1931, he said, "What I most admire about your art is its universality. You don't say a word, yet the world understands you." He said, "It's true, but your fame is even greater! The world admires you when no one understands you." A tiny and physically weak person thus became a world visionary from the bunch of ordinary people by sheer courage and mental toughness.

Conclusion

This small book is all about ordinary people whom the world throws out in the waste basket to neglect and perish. This book is an awakening call to all of them. Just to receive the call and do your best for beginning a new era/ chapter of your life. Good luck to all of you.